Searchlight BOOKS™

Fear Fest

Spooky

Haunted Houses

Tracy Nelson Maurer

Lerner Publications • Minneapolis

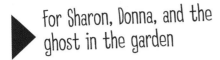

For Sharon, Donna, and the
ghost in the garden

Lerner Publications Company
A division of Lerner Publishing Group, Inc.
241 First Avenue North
Minneapolis, MN 55401 USA

For reading levels and more information, look up this title
at www.lernerbooks.com.

Library of Congress Cataloging-in-Publication Data

The Cataloging-in-Publication Data for *Spooky Haunted Houses* is on file at the Library
of Congress.
ISBN 978-1-5124-3401-9 (lib. bdg.)
ISBN 978-1-5124-5608-0 (pbk.)
ISBN 978-1-5124-5079-8 (EB pdf)

LC record available at https://lccn.loc.gov/2016046975

Manufactured in the United States of America
1-42037-23907-12/27/2016

Contents

Chapter 1

WHAT MAKES A HOUSE HAUNTED?

If you saw a spooky old house at night on a hilltop guarded by spindly oaks, would you climb the rickety front steps . . . and push open the creeeaky front door? Would you step inside and wait in the dark with the spiderwebs, mice, and bats for the chance to see a ghost? That's one way to find a haunted house!

Some would say this rickety old house is haunted, but others don't believe in hauntings. What's one reason believers give for why a ghost might haunt a house?

What (or Who) Haunts a House?

Most people who claim a house is haunted think a ghost is behind the haunting. They believe ghosts are the souls of people who have died but remain on Earth. Most often in ghost stories, a spirit haunts the place where it once lived—and where it died. Those who believe in ghosts often say that ghosts can't let go of their former homes. Perhaps they have unfinished business there. Or maybe the ghost just loved its house so much that it doesn't want to leave!

Cemeteries are prime ghost-hunting spots.

The White House looks bright and stately by daylight, but some are sure it's haunted.

Which Houses Are Haunted?

Crumbling old castles and dusty mansions seem to inspire the most haunted house stories. But some haunted houses are well kept, and families still live in them—such as the White House in Washington, DC.

That's right! Did you know the White House is said to be haunted? Almost every first family, including the Obamas, has reported hearing spine-tingling sounds at night or seeing ghosts in the rooms. Abraham Lincoln is the most frequently reported ghost. Besides houses, other haunted places include hospitals, prisons, lighthouses, hotels, and apartments. But really, almost any place can be haunted. All it needs is a ghost!

fact or fiction?

A ghost is the same as a spirit, phantom, poltergeist, apparition, or specter . . . right?

That's a fact—almost.

A ghost is thought to be a wandering soul, and it can also be called a spirit or a phantom. *Poltergeist* means "noisy ghost" in German. This kind of invisible ghost moves objects or makes noises. Apparitions and specters are visible ghosts. Specters are believed to be extra-menacing ghosts. You don't want one of these ghouls haunting your place!

Ghosts terrorize a child in this scene from the movie *Poltergeist*.

A Mysterious Home

One of the most famous haunted places in the United States is the Winchester Mystery House near San Jose, California. Sarah Winchester bought the partially built farmhouse in 1884. For the next thirty-eight years, the wealthy widow had carpenters work around the clock to add on to the house. The project may have been a distraction from Winchester's grief over losing both her husband and infant daughter to serious illnesses.

Sarah Winchester herself is mysterious! Rarely photographed, Winchester appears here in the only known picture of her in existence.

Over the years, workers built and rebuilt as many as 600 rooms onto the house! These days, the home has 160 rooms and is said to have many hauntings. Countless sightings of ghostly builders, servants, and Mrs. Winchester herself have been reported. Would *you* dare enter the Winchester Mystery House?

Two large stone statues greet daring visitors to the Winchester Mystery House.

Chapter 2

HOW OLD ARE GHOST STORIES?

Before written words, most cultures passed ghost stories from generation to generation by sharing them aloud. Such stories go all the way back to ancient times. From the Egyptians and Chinese to the ancient Greeks and Brits, nearly all cultures have spooky stories that have spread and evolved through the years. Gathering around a bonfire to share haunted tales has long been a popular pastime.

Telling ghost stories around a campfire is a time-honored practice. But do you know when spooky stories first became popular?

Haunted History

Most ghost stories are about ghouls that haunt physical places—so ghost stories are inseparable from haunted houses. Haunted house tales, perhaps surprisingly, have a very merry past. They first became popular in the mid-nineteenth century as part of Christmas celebrations in England and the United States!

In mid-nineteenth-century England, ghost tales were as much a part of Christmas as cutting down a tree.

One very popular ghost story from the past even has Christmas as its subject. You may have heard the tale of ghosts from the past, present, and future who haunted old Ebenezer Scrooge in his home as he tried to sleep in *A Christmas Carol*. Charles Dickens wrote the story in 1843 to urge people to think more kindly about their neighbors, especially those in need. He once said he hoped the story would "haunt" people in a good way—by sticking with them so that they always remembered to treat others well.

The ghost of Scrooge's business partner Jacob Marley haunts Scrooge in this drawing from *A Christmas Carol*.

fact or fiction?

Charles Dickens was one of the nineteenth century's best spooky storytellers.

That's a fact!

Dickens may be well known for not-so-terrifying tales such as *Oliver Twist* and *Great Expectations*. But *A Christmas Carol* was far from the only frightening story Dickens penned. The famous author wrote more than twenty ghost tales in the nineteenth century. He even joined London's Ghost Club, an early paranormal research group founded in 1862. All things scary simply fascinated him!

These days, some people claim to see the ghost of Charles Dickens in London. Dickens would probably love the ghost stories that have been told about him.

Charles Dickens

The Victorian era (1837–1901) in general was rich with tales of haunted places. This era brought many stories about fairies and witches as well as good old-fashioned ghosts. These spooky figures often followed humans around, making noises, moving objects, and doing anything else they could think of to disturb the peace.

As you can see, stories having to do with hauntings go way back. People in the past just loved to be scared. And people still do. This explains why stories about haunted houses have remained so popular through the years.

An apparition pays a visit to a startled man in this Victorian illustration.

Chapter 3

WHO HUNTS FOR HAUNTED HOUSES?

As long as there have been tales about haunted houses, there have been people living in those houses who didn't want to room with a ghost! People who believe their house is haunted usually want to get to the bottom of whatever is causing the disturbances. Enter ghost hunters.

Ghost hunters are also known as paranormal investigators. Their goal is to find out what's going on in haunted places.

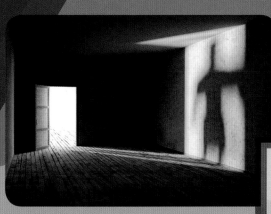

Boo! What's the name for someone who investigates haunted places?

The Tower of London looks mysterious even in broad daylight!

ENTRY TO THE TRAITORS GATE

Super-Spooky Places

Ghost hunters travel the world to chase stories of haunted houses. Some places tend to attract more reports than others. The Tower of London in England ranks as one of the most famous supposedly haunted sites. Built around the year 1067, this stone fortress has been a palace, a prison, and home to the crown jewels. Reports of ghosts began in the mid-thirteenth century. Visitors and workers there still claim that ghosts of murdered royalty, executed prisoners, and even children haunt the place.

Do some people really find fame by hunting ghosts—besides in the *Ghostbusters* movies?

Believe it or not, it's a fact that some ghost hunters have become extremely famous.

Wondering where you might go to find out about famous ghost hunters? For starters, turn on the TV. Well-known ghost hunters work on television shows such as *Ghost Adventures* and *Ghost Hunters*. You can also find famous ghost hunters through social media and websites. Many paranormal investigators have found a following by posting their ghost-hunting adventures online. Still others write books about ghost hunting.

Ghost Hunters (*left*) is a very popular show.

Ghostly Clues

When ghost hunters go into a place like the Tower of London, they look for certain clues. Here's some of what they search for:

- a history of tragic or mysterious death
- faraway voices, eerie laughter, moans and cries, or howling
- strange tapping, scratching, rattling, or thumping noises
- unexplained images of people in mirrors, windows, or photographs
- lights, music, radios, televisions, or other electronics turning on or off
- unusual odors
- hot or cold spots

Who knows what phantoms are lurking near this window? It looks like a job for ghost hunters!

This walkway in an old abandoned building seems like a likely haunt for ghosts.

The Ghost Hunt

Ghost hunters learn about a building's normal conditions before they launch a stakeout. They want to know what a place's usual temperatures, sounds, and lighting are like. This makes it easier to spot what is unusual.

Most stakeouts happen after dark, often in damp or dusty rooms. Investigators work in teams for safety. A team also means more witnesses to any ghostly events.

Only the team members enter a building for a stakeout. They set up special equipment, such as a camera to snap pictures of ghost sightings, a video recorder to capture motion, and an audio recorder to pick up any unusual sounds. Then they wait.

VIDEO CAMERAS EQUIPPED WITH MICS ARE A CRITICAL TOOL FOR GHOST HUNTERS.

The four main characters of the 2016 *Ghostbusters* movie aren't afraid to meet ghosts head on!

Stakeouts take a lot of patience. Sometimes a whole night goes by where nothing happens. But to ghost hunters, the wait is worth it—because sometimes they spot something interesting.

Ghost hunters have caught such things as doors slamming shut by themselves, spooky-sounding noises, and even what appeared to be actual ghosts. No one has been able to prove these incidents were really caused by ghosts. But then again, no one has been able to entirely disprove it either. As long as there are unusual events for ghost hunters to witness, there will always be jobs for those who hunt ghosts!

Chapter 4

WILL WE EVER REALLY KNOW?

If even professional ghost hunters haven't been able to prove that some places are haunted, then can we ever truly know if haunted houses are real? It's hard to say for sure. But researchers interested in reports of haunted places have some ways to investigate the reports. Perhaps their methods will one day lead us to conclusions about places where things go bump in the night!

Researchers dig into reports of places said to be haunted. What is one method they use?

Haunting History

One method researchers use to examine reports of hauntings is to look at the history of each report. For example, they look into how many people have reported the same experience over time. If only one person claimed to hear spooky noises in a hotel's dining room at night, it could be that the person mistook the kitchen staff's chitchat for otherworldly communication! If, on the other hand, *hundreds* of hotel guests have heard mysterious noises, there's a stronger case that something spooky's going on.

Many guests at the Hotel Colorado in Glenwood Springs, Colorado (*below*), have reported hearing spooky noises there. Is it haunted? Maybe it is, and maybe it isn't!

Reviewing Results

Researchers also look closely at the results from any stakeouts performed by ghost hunters. Does a photo show a ghost? Or could it simply be curtains blowing in the wind in a shape that sort of *looks* like a ghost? Is that a specter running across the floor in that video? Or could it just be a cat that's running so fast it looks like a mysterious blur?

Sometimes it can be really hard to tell what's going on in an image. For example, a family named the Coopers posed for a photo after moving into a new home in Texas in the 1950s. When they looked at the photo, they saw what appeared to be a body hanging above them! In this case, no one's ever been able to get to the bottom of what's happening in that picture.

What do you think is really going on in this photo of a ghostly-looking shape?

The sounds of people chatting can carry through apartment walls—but some say the sounds of ghosts can too!

Researchers listen especially carefully to audio recordings from stakeouts. They listen for electronic voice phenomena (EVP). EVP are mysterious-sounding voices. Most often, no one hears the voices during the stakeout. But when the recording is played back, it reveals EVPs such as grunts, groans, whispered names, or short sentences. Researchers consider whether there could be a logical explanation for the EVPs. Could a groan be the wind blowing softly outside a window? Could a whispered name be chatter from the hallway in the apartment building where the stakeout took place?

Seeing for Themselves

Researchers can also pay an in-person visit to a site that's said to be haunted. They might talk to people who live nearby and ask if they've noticed anything strange. They could look for physical causes behind any odd phenomena people have reported. In-person investigations can be one of the best ways to find out more about a spooky place.

If researchers ever caught a specter like this one, they would need to investigate no further!

Fact or Fiction?

Your family could buy a famous haunted house.

Fact! Although it's up to you to decide if the famous house is really haunted.

Houses said to be haunted really do go up for sale. A very well-known home where hauntings supposedly happened went up for sale in 2016. The home is known as the Amityville Horror House. It's in Amityville, New York. Ronald DeFeo Jr. and his family were living there in 1974 when DeFeo murdered his parents and four siblings while they slept. He claimed voices told him to do it. Ever since the killings, ghostly voices and a whole host of paranormal events have supposedly been witnessed at the house. Would *you* dare move in?

The Amityville Horror House inspired a 1977 book called *The Amityville Horror*. Two years later, a movie by the same name hit the theaters.

Whether we get to the bottom of the mystery behind haunted houses or not, learning more about hauntings can be a lot of fun. And if you believe in haunted houses, then who knows? Perhaps one day, *you'll* be the one to discover the truth about the secrets they hold. Until then, the spooky legends live on.

Is this crumbling house haunted, or just a run-of-the-mill old home? You be the judge!

Believe It or Not!

- Friendly ghosts have been reported to give tours of their homes, theaters, and other favorite haunts. They're not as exciting as evil spirits, so you don't hear much about them.

- Ghosts can be animals. For example, ghost dogs are said to haunt the pet cemetery at Scotland's Edinburgh Castle.

- You can actually stay at some haunted places, such as hotels or bed-and-breakfasts that have a reputation for providing ghostly visits.

Glossary

apparition: a visible ghost

electronic voice phenomena (EVP): mysterious voices detected in a recording

paranormal: beyond normal scientific understanding

poltergeist: an invisible ghost that moves objects or makes noises

specter: a type of visible ghost thought to be especially menacing

stakeout: standing watch over a place to look for a certain kind of activity. Ghost hunters conduct stakeouts to look for paranormal activity.

Learn More about Haunted Houses

Books

Everett, J. H., and Marilyn Scott-Waters. *Haunted Histories: Creepy Castles, Dark Dungeons, and Powerful Palaces*. New York: Henry Holt, 2012. A tween "ghostorian" takes readers on a wild tour of haunted castles, dungeons, and more in this fun title.

Kallio, Jamie. *Haunted Houses*. Mankato, MN: Child's World, 2015. Learn more about spooky places in this book on haunted houses.

Vega, Ali. *Witches' Brew and Other Horrifying Party Foods*. Minneapolis: Lerner Publications, 2017. If you like all things creepy, then you'll love this book about how to whip up some hauntingly good treats for your next party.

Websites

About: Ghost Hunting
http://paranormal.about.com/od/ghosthuntinggeninfo
Check out this fun page to learn everything you've ever wanted to know about ghost hunting.

History: Ghosts in the White House
http://www.history.com/topics/halloween/ghosts-in-the-white-house
Read this article about hauntings at the United States' most famous address.

Houdini Museum
http://houdini.net/museum
Famous magician Harry Houdini loved mysterious things. Visit the home page of his museum in Scranton, Pennsylvania, to find pictures, video clips, and more having to do with Houdini and all things mysterious!

Index

Photo Acknowledgments

The images in this book are used with the permission of: © Marafona/Shutterstock.com, p. 4; © Peter Cripps/Shutterstock.com, p. 5; © Orhan Cam/Shutterstock.com, p. 6; © AF Archive/Alamy, pp. 7, 27; © Bettmann/Getty Images, p. 8; © Citizen of the Planet/Alamy, p. 9; © Volodya Senkiv/Shutterstock.com, p. 10; © North Wind Picture Archive/Alamy, p. 11; © Lordprice Collection/Alamy, p. 12; © GL Archive/Alamy, p. 13; © iStockphoto.com/YaroslavGerzhedovich, p. 14; © Igor Iakovlev/Shutterstock.com, p. 15; © Salpardis/Shutterstock.com, p. 16; © Alan David Management/Pilgrim Films and TV/REX/Shutterstock, p. 17; © iStockphoto.com/belterz, p. 18; © waewkid/Shutterstock.com, p. 19; © nikkytok/Shutterstock.com, p. 20; © Columbia Pictures/Feigco Entertainment/REX/Shutterstock, p. 21; © iStockphoto.com/photka, p. 22; © Blaine Harrington III/Alamy, p. 23; © Renphoto/Shutterstock.com, p. 24; © Stephen Orsillo/Shutterstock.com, p. 25; © Artokolor Quint Lox Limited/Alamy, p. 26; © Kimberly Palmer/Shutterstock.com, p. 28.

Front cover: © Maksim Shmeljov/Shutterstock.com (background), © Razvan Ionut Dragomirescu/Shutterstock.com.

Main body text set in Adrianna Regular 14/20.
Typeface provided by Chank.